W9-AHJ-203

be mindful

Plant the Seeds of Clarity, Wisdom, and Compassion

pil
Publications International, Ltd.

Contributing writer: Marie D. Jones

Cover art: Shutterstock.com

Interior art: Art Explosion: 81, 215; **Artville:** 12, 31, 36, 96, 105, 108, 109, 145, 153, 179, 184, 198, 210; Corbis: 5, 112, 166, 199; **Getty:** 8, 10, 14, 15, 16, 17, 18, 23, 27, 28, 29, 30, 33, 34, 43, 45, 47, 54, 56, 57, 58, 60, 61, 62, 65, 67, 78, 80, 82, 83, 84, 86, 88, 90, 94, 95, 99, 102, 104, 106, 110, 114, 118, 119, 120, 121, 122, 123, 124, 125, 129, 134, 140, 142, 142, 146, 149, 159, 160, 163, 168, 169, 172, 174, 176, 181, 182, 186, 190, 192, 195, 196, 203, 204, 208, 212, 213, 214, 218, 220, 222, 223, 224, 226, 236, 237, 238, 240, 246, 250, 253, 254, 255, 256; **Shutterstock.com:** 4, 6, 7, 9, 11, 13, 21, 22, 24, 25, 26, 32, 35, 37, 38, 40, 42, 45, 46, 48, 49, 50, 55, 64, 66, 68, 69, 70, 71, 73, 74, 75, 77, 79, 85, 87, 91, 92, 93, 97, 98, 100, 101, 107, 111, 113, 115, 116, 117, 126, 127, 130, 131, 135, 136, 137, 141, 143, 144, 150, 151, 152, 154, 155, 156, 157, 158, 161, 162, 164, 165, 167, 170, 171, 173, 175, 177, 178, 183, 183, 187, 188, 191, 193, 194, 197, 200, 202, 205, 206, 209, 211, 216, 217, 219, 219, 221, 225, 227, 228, 229, 230, 231, 232, 234, 235, 239, 241, 242, 243, 247, 248, 251

Louis Weber, CEO
Publications International, Ltd.
7373 North Cicero Avenue
Lincolnwood, Illinois 60712

ISBN: 978-1-68022-319-4

Manufactured in China.

8 7 6 5 4 3 2 1

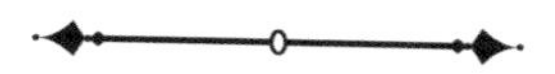

Modern life seems to grow more hectic each day, and it's no surprise that people around the world have embraced mindfulness meditation. This technique sounds deceptively simple—"All I have to do is sit still?"—but requires practice, an open mind, and a quiet place to sit.

Much of what we think of as *mindfulness* originates in Hinduism and Buddhism, but the practice of meditation dates back millennia to the ancient religious beliefs of many groups. Contemplation is one of the human species' unique higher capacities, and even the word "mindfulness" evokes the awareness, abstract thinking, and inner world that the human brain enables us to have. What a biological novelty: to have such complex thinking that you need a way to quiet some of those thoughts!

Many spiritual traditions have some kind of altered consciousness, from the whirling dervishes of Sufi Islam to the glossolalia of Pentecostal Christianity. But mindfulness in the secular sense is not religious—it may be spiritual for you, and it's very personal, but no special belief or adherence is required. Rhythmic breathing and redirected thinking patterns, much like yoga, are suggested to reduce stress and anxiety. Think of it like an emergency dose of vitamin "calm."

Maybe you've thought for a long time that you admire a friend or family member who attributes their calmness to meditation. Maybe you're simply ready to turn off your electronic life for a few minutes and try to tune out your thoughts of work and family obligations. In this book you'll find simple meditation prompts, anecdotes, and other material to inspire your mindfulness practice. There's no downside to giving it a try, no equipment or fee required.

Imagine reducing anxiety with meditation, not medication. Studies show that even ten minutes of mindful meditation a day can calm the mind and create a tranquil state that decreases both anxiety and depression. These dramatic effects to the body, mind, and spirit last for the rest of the day, no yoga or pilgrimage required.

Meditation is not hard. What is hard is finding the time for it. Start small, with five minute increments of quiet time. Build up to ten minutes, then twenty. Before long, meditation will be easy. Not meditating will be hard.

Find a place to sit comfortably free from distractions. Turn off all gadgets. Breathe in and out deeply. Focus on the movement of breath into and out of the lungs. Stay still for at least ten minutes. When thoughts interrupt, let them pass like clouds. Take a breath and imagine gently blowing the thoughts away.

Take a breath. Visualize the air as a color. The color is blue, filling you with peace. Take another breath, filling your lungs with pink, for love. Now breathe yellow, for harmony and oneness. Relax and breathe in orange, for energy and vitality. Inhale white, for union with the divine. Hold the breath for five seconds, letting the color spread to every cell, muscle, bone, and vital organ.

I do not resist the thoughts that pass through my mind. I lovingly acknowledge them and gently move past them to the stillness within. I rest in that stillness, doing nothing, being nothing, wanting nothing. Thoughts arise. I love them away and become more still.

There is light within me. There is love throughout me. I breathe in light and release darkness from my body and my spirit. I breathe in positive energy, and release all that is negative. I invite the present into my thoughts and allow spirit to order my day. I am filled with light inward. I am expressing love outward.

Being mindful means being completely present to the feelings, sensations, and experiences of the moment. It means putting away watches and phones and devices and tuning into nature or the sound of your own breath. It means having no sense of worry, need, fear, demand, or expectation of what should be and instead allowing life to unfold as is.

Mindfulness requires no equipment or membership. You only need:

- A quiet place free from interruptions
- Music, a guided meditation, or pure silence
- The ability to sit still for at least ten minutes
- To experience what is, without resistance
- Patience to focus and center your breathing
- The desire to live a more balanced, harmonious life

I let the world melt away, surrendering only to the moment I exist in right now. There is nothing more than my breath moving into my lungs and moving out again. I am no longer solid, heavy, but light and free of encumbrances. My mind floats upward and outward, becoming one with the sky. My spirit takes flight then floats downward. I open my eyes, returned home.

Close your eyes now and repeat to yourself: “I am here, now. I am here, now.” Allow the chaos of the day to drift away on the ocean of your conscious awareness. “I am here, now.” Let go of what weighs you down in body and in spirit. “I am here, now.” Be here, now.

Buddhist traditions use meditation to relax, to restore health, and to experience altered consciousness. The mind, when still, opens up to a more cosmic connection and an expansion of self.

Meditation is not about merely feeling calm, but feeling whole and experiencing the grandness and majesty of being alive. It's a human and spiritual practice that benefits the body as well as the soul.

As soon as I notice I am worrying about the future, or regretting the past, I quiet my mind and bring it back to the present moment. I allow the feeling of calmness and clarity to wash over me. I breathe in the "now" and breathe out any concerns of "then." Centered, I continue with my day.

Discovering she had breast cancer was life-altering. The initial fear crippled Angie with worry. Would she see her daughter get married? Should she change her goals: success in her career, running a marathon? She had gone from believing she was whole and healthy to dreading a future she wasn't even sure she should plan.

The power of mindfulness saved Angie as much as treatment did. During the long haul of surgeries, radiation, and reconstruction, she kept meditating every morning and letting her thoughts melt away. In the present moment, she was healthy and strong and invincible. In the now, she was whole. She is now a survivor—a thriver.

Each moment of life is a meditation. I am mindful of the present as I go about my day. I stay centered and grounded in the calm within, no matter what goes on outside me. I acknowledge life unfolding around me and offer no resistance to what is. I am here. I am now.

Forgiveness blesses us in so many ways:

- Vanquishes anger's stranglehold on us
- Gives us back responsibility for our own lives
- Opens us up to love and trust again
- Lightens our mental load of worry and anxiety
- Dissipates resentments and dismantles grudges
- Sets us free from the cage of the past

Upon awakening, I think of all I am grateful for. Before I sleep, I think of all I am grateful for. My mind begins and ends in a state of peace, harmony and presence, and I allow the hours between the beginning and the end to flow without resistance.

My mind is in a quiet place deep
in nature, warmed by an inner sun.
A gentle breeze moves across my body.
Eyes closed, I allow myself to be in this
magical place, with no expectations or
goals. I become both the warm sun and
the gentle breeze. I am at one with my
surroundings. I am at peace.

The breath is your healing power. Breathe in the white healing light. Let it wash over the unwellness in your body, restoring it to balance. Exhale illness and inhale strength. With each new breath, feel yourself empowered and renewed. Let the rhythm of your breathing be like the ocean waves, taking out sickness, bringing in wholeness.

Before you rise to face the day, sit quietly for five minutes and think about someone in your life you are grateful for. Focus the mind on the feeling of gratitude, and the love you feel for this person. Breathe deeply, letting that sense of gratefulness expand like the ripples in a pond to everyone around you. Now, go face the day with a full heart and a happy spirit.

The gentle breeze softly caressing my face
The softness of a sweater draped around my shoulders
Sounds of nature filling the empty spaces in my mind
Nourishing breath moving in and out of my lungs
Sweet calm washing away the chaos of the day

In the stillness of the night, I calm my spirit with this mantra: "I am all there is." I speak the words quietly in rhythm with my breathing, allowing them to heal my anxious mind. All is well in this moment. All is well in this centered place. I am all there is, and I am complete in the here and the now.

I find my quiet center and ground myself. There, I remember a time in my childhood when I felt free. I let my body absorb the feeling of freedom, of joy, playing in the grass with no cares or concerns. I am laughing, running, smelling the flowers in the garden. I melt into this memory, and I am a child again.

"Above all, we cannot afford not to live in the present. He is blessed over all mortals who loses no moment of the passing life in remembering the past. It is an expression of the health and soundness of Nature, a brag for all the world—healthiness as of a spring burst forth, a new fountain of the Muses."

— Henry David Thoreau

Focus the mind on one thing: perhaps the breath, perhaps a mantra, perhaps gentle music or a beautiful landscape. Keeping the mind in the moment, free of past and future concerns, is the cornerstone of meditation. Focus on anything that helps to quiet you and brings a feeling of inner and outer calm.

Don't worry about sitting in the proper position, or putting your hands in the right place. Meditation requires only that you be present and relaxed. That could be riding a horse through a field or sitting on the dock of a peaceful lake with your feet in the water. Find a place to be present and a position that feels comfortable. Now lose yourself.

What makes you happy? Envision one thing that brings you joy and let that be the focus of your meditation today. Free the mind of everything but the love you feel, whether for a person, place, or object. Immerse yourself in appreciation and gratitude for this beloved presence. This simple practice opens the heart to the wonders of your daily life.

How often do you stop and think about what you're thinking? Slow down and quiet the mind. Observe the thoughts that move in and out of your mind. Are they mostly negative? Positive? Empowering, or disempowering? Meditation allows you to become aware of your mind chatter and ultimately think better, clearer thoughts.

A bird in flight is a meditation in beauty and freedom: lifting, diving, floating on air. A bird sometimes flies to find food or shelter, but sometimes just for the sheer joy of it. With wings spread to catch cloud and sun and sky, a bird has no limits, no hindrances—just a moment upon the wind, soaring. The mind is a bird in flight.

"The world is full of the talk of love, but it is hard to love. Where is love? How do you know that there is love? The first test of love is that it knows no bargaining. So long as you see a man love another only to get something from him, you know that that is not love; it is shopkeeping."

— Swami Vivekenanda

Joy is fleeting and elusive. Meditate on joy and allow yourself to truly feel the freedom and abandon that comes from letting go of all that weighs you down. Let each breath take you higher and make you lighter until you are nothing but pure joyful energy with no limitations or constraints.

Breath is life. When we breathe in, we bring life-giving nutrients into our bodies. Breath is spirit. Following the rhythm of the breath deepens our connection to our spirit and changes our consciousness. Breath is peace. A mind free of chatter, but focused on the breath, is serene.

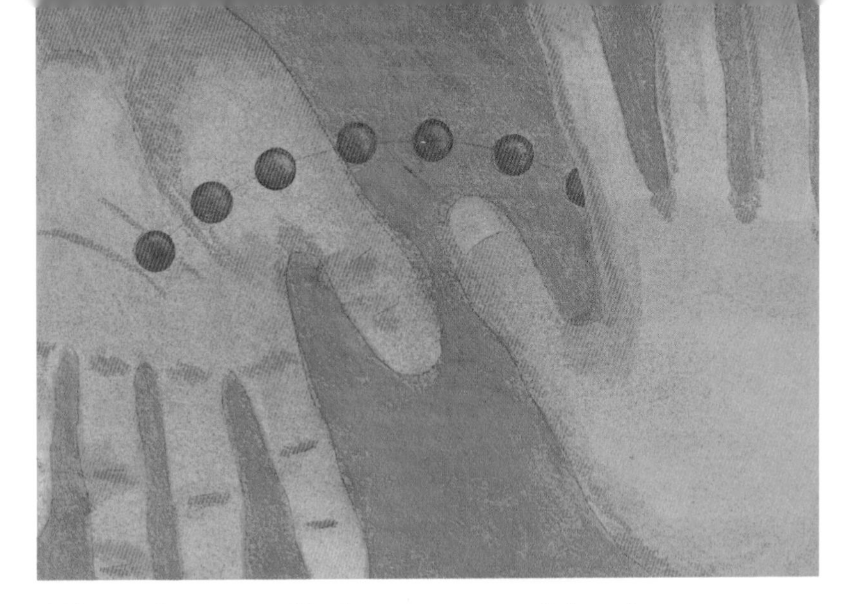

All my dreams of being a successful writer were coming true. I had deals and contracts and, with those, expectations and demands. Soon, I felt anxious and filled with doubts. A friend suggested present-moment meditations, and I laughed. Writers don't know how to still the mind! Our thoughts never cease.

But I needed to get control of the rising panic and tried five minutes one morning, doing nothing more than breathing in and out. Thoughts invaded, and I acknowledged them and returned to my breathing. When I opened my eyes, twenty minutes had passed. I felt calm and a reassuring sense of being right where I needed to be. I now start every day this way and feel ready for any challenge.

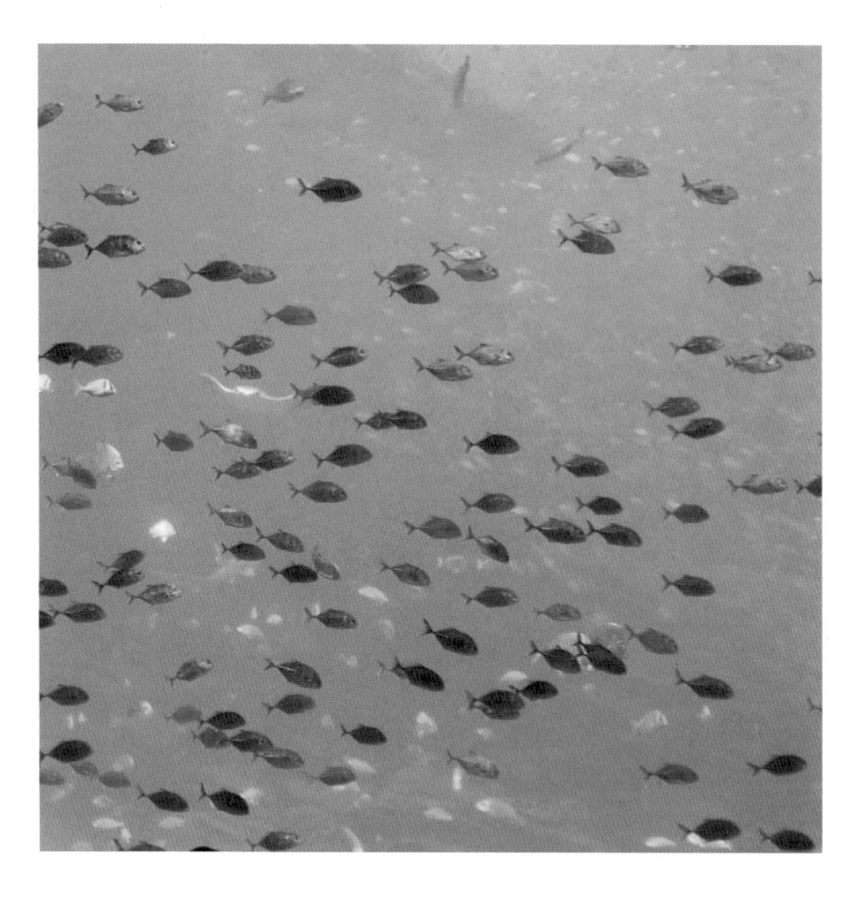

I go within to find the center of my being. Here, I rest a while, feeling at peace. In this moment, my mind is awake and aware. Nothing external bothers or distracts me. I am focused. At my center, there is only now, only this experience of this moment. I am calm. I am open. I am free.

"What we say a man 'knows,' should, in strict psychological language, be what he 'discovers' or 'unveils'; what man 'learns' is really what he discovers by taking the cover off his own soul, which is a mine of infinite knowledge."

— Swami Vivekenanda

Visualize a lovely bench at the edge of a field of wildflowers. Sit down, in your mind, and look at the colors spread across the field like a painter's palette. Feel the sun and the breeze and relax, basking in the warmth and beauty of nature. Listen to birds in the trees bordering the field. Stay here awhile, among the flowers, among the birds.

My mind is like a jar of water, pouring out, emptying into the greater sea of consciousness. Now empty, I fill my mind with light. I let the light overflow and expand outward, glowing, warming. I focus on the light and let myself bask in the glow of pure love and positive energy. My mind becomes the light.

Mindfulness is paying attention to the here and now. It is not about denying feelings or experiences, but being fully present with them, whether good or bad. It's about reducing our struggle against what is and what will be and instead accepting it. Through it, we both enjoy happiness more and alleviate our suffering.

Choose a comfortable place to meditate and make it your own. It could be a soft pillow, your bed, or a recliner. It could be indoors or outdoors—free of loud distractions. Let your family know that this is your alone time and your quiet place. Make it a place you'll look forward returning to again as you learn to let go and go within.

"The powers of the mind should be concentrated and the mind turned back upon itself; as the darkest places reveal their secrets before the penetrating rays of the sun, so will the concentrated mind penetrate its own innermost secrets."

— Swami Vivekenanda

Counting backward from ten to one, let your mind become more and more quiet and calm. Breathe in with each count, holding the breath for three seconds before exhaling to the count of three. Feel your entire being relax into the pureness of the moment at hand. Breathe deeply for ten minutes: surrendering, allowing.

With each breath, I slow the march of thoughts in my mind. With each breath, my body relaxes and I welcome the calm of the present. With each breath, I let go of stress and worry, inhaling peace. My being is centered, grounded, and serene. With each breath, I release the concerns of the day.

In meditation, I am the observer. I step away from my thoughts and see them without judgment or reaction. I am relaxed as I let them drift across the screen of my mind. I clearly see my thoughts and how they affect me. I stay calm and let go of what doesn't serve me.

"If the mind gets to the centre,
you begin to be conscious
on all planes. In meditation
sometimes you touch another
plane, and you see other beings,
disembodied spirits, and so on.
You get there by the power
of meditation. This power is
changing our senses, you see,
refining our senses."

— Swami Vivekenanda

Dance is meditation in action. Feel each muscle gracefully relax and contract. Hear the music deep within the soul. Move in rhythm to the resonating sound of breath and body. Allow the dance to become the expansion of mind and the physical form. Be aware, and dance that awareness into being.

At the center of my being there is no time, no past, present, or future. Time does not exist here, only breath and being and awareness. I am in no hurry. I rest and relax and simply experience myself. Now I am ageless, timeless, and formless. In the center of my being, I am one with everything.

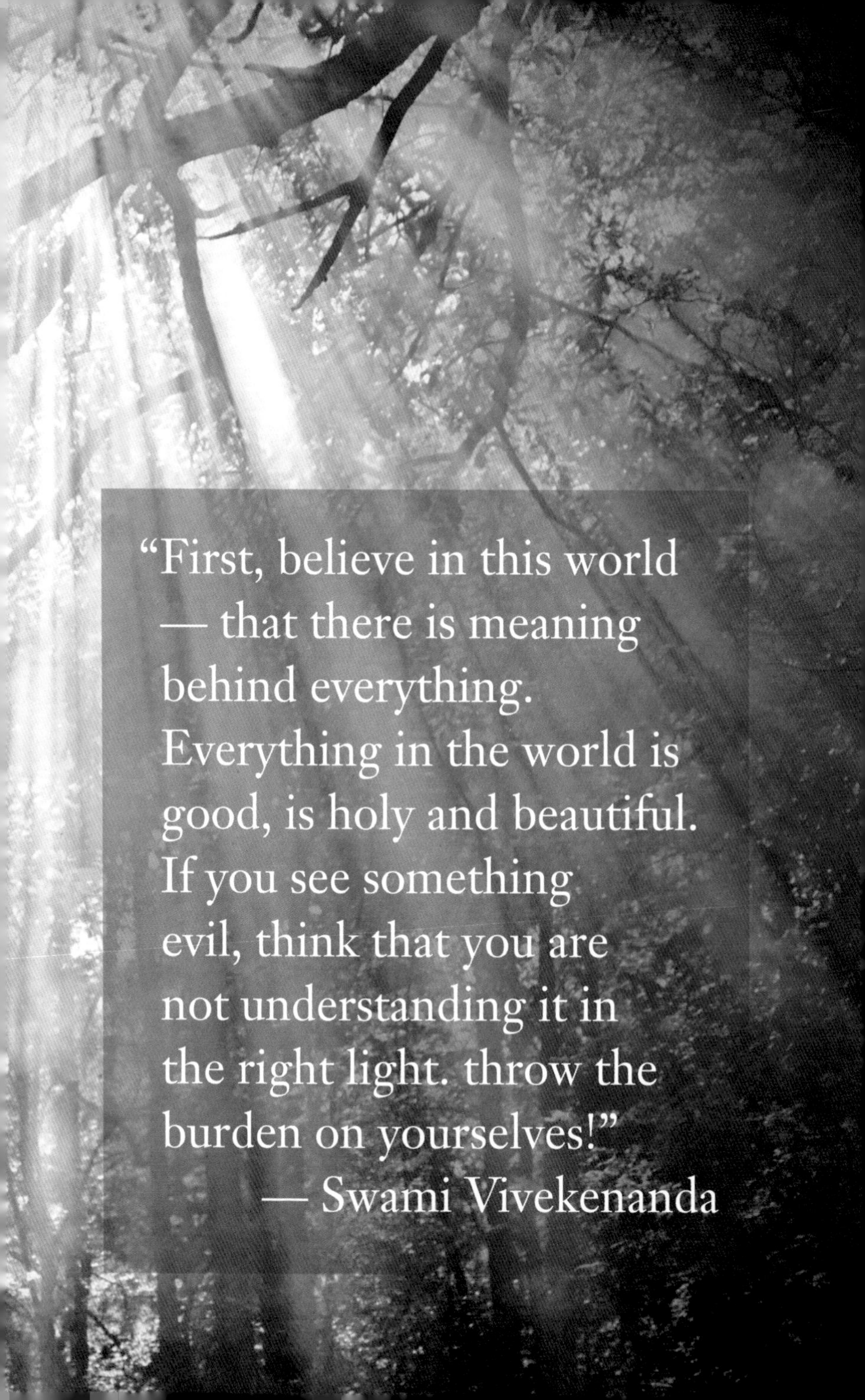
"First, believe in this world
— that there is meaning
behind everything.
Everything in the world is
good, is holy and beautiful.
If you see something
evil, think that you are
not understanding it in
the right light. throw the
burden on yourselves!"
— Swami Vivekenanda

Guided meditations are brief spiritual journeys for the mind and soul. I am free to focus on the sound of another's voice and simply follow, letting my imagination take me wherever I am directed. I need not worry about doing it right. I simply listen, relaxed, and let go of all distractions. I journey within.

The beauty and wonder of nature is meditative. Spend some time absorbing the healing rays of the sun. Listen to birdsong and lose yourself in the gentle breezes. Walk barefoot on the soft grass. Notice your worries melt away from the warmth of the sun on your skin. Just as the tree is rooted deep inside the earth, ground yourself and reach your arms to the sky. Breathe in healing and peace.

Pause midstream in the activity of your day and close your eyes. Breathe in through your nose, hold the breath for a count of five, then gently and slowly exhale. Do this three times and feel the stress and chaos of the first part of the day disappear. Open your eyes and face the rest of the day, calm and centered.

"Let positive, strong, helpful thoughts enter into your brains from very childhood. Lay yourselves open to these thoughts, and not to weakening and paralysing ones."

— Swami Vivekenanda

"Thousands of divine beings are standing about you. You do not see them because our world is determined by our senses. Let us take the tree standing outside. A thief came and what did he see in the stump? A policeman. The child saw a huge ghost. The young man was waiting for his sweetheart, and what did he see? His sweetheart. But the stump of the tree had not changed. It remained the same."

— Swami Vivekenanda

Listen to the laughter of children, and watch them as they play. Children live in the present and it is there they find joy and wonder. Move your mind into the present moment and dwell there for a while, feeling that playful sense of joy rising within you. Empty your mind of grown-up worries and be light and free and filled with wonder like a child.

Do you notice how the gravity of fear and anxiety weighs down the mind? Free your mind by breathing deeply into just this moment, where fear and anxiety have no foothold. Just this moment . . . and breathe. Just this moment, and breathe again. Repeat when necessary.

In the present moment, the mind has a chance to be free to create, to heal, and to offer wisdom.

Use a journal to write down breakthrough ideas and insights that come once the active brain is settled and the creative mind awakens.

After my divorce, I struggled with loneliness. I didn't want to jump into dating right away but felt so alone. I began meditating each morning and letting my ego fade away. Focused on the sounds of birds outside my window, I felt a sense of oneness and expansion.

The more I did this, the more I realized I was not alone. I sensed a loving presence at the core of my being, there for me whenever I needed it. I felt like part of everything around me. I'm sure one day I will date again, but for now, my time alone in meditation keeps me connected to life in a deeper, more satisfying sense.

Sounds, sights, and smells can bring us back to special places and times in our lives.

- The nightsong of crickets outside the window
- The distant whistle of a passing train
- The alluring scent of night-blooming jasmine
- The taste of salt on the lips from the ocean waves
- The steady beat of summer rain

Still the mind and let consciousness shift. Sense the oneness with all that exists. Become a part of that oneness, that wholeness. Let go of the beliefs in boundaries that separate you from that oneness. Merge with it, allowing it to fill your mind, heart, and spirit. You are connected with everything. One with all there is. Here in that oneness, all is well. You are whole.

The breath of life nourishes and sustains me. I grow still, breathing in air that fills me with energy. Oxygen wends into my limbs and my core. I sink deeply into my connection with my body. I reside there, not doing but being. I relax there.

Don't just look at something—see it, feel it, and imagine being it. Remember that everyone you meet has a story to tell.

When someone looks at you, engage with a smile. Notice little things you usually pass over, like the flowers in a neighbor's yard.

Pause to feel the breeze on your skin or the sun on your face. Do one thing at a time so you may focus and be mindful.

Be present for yourself and others.

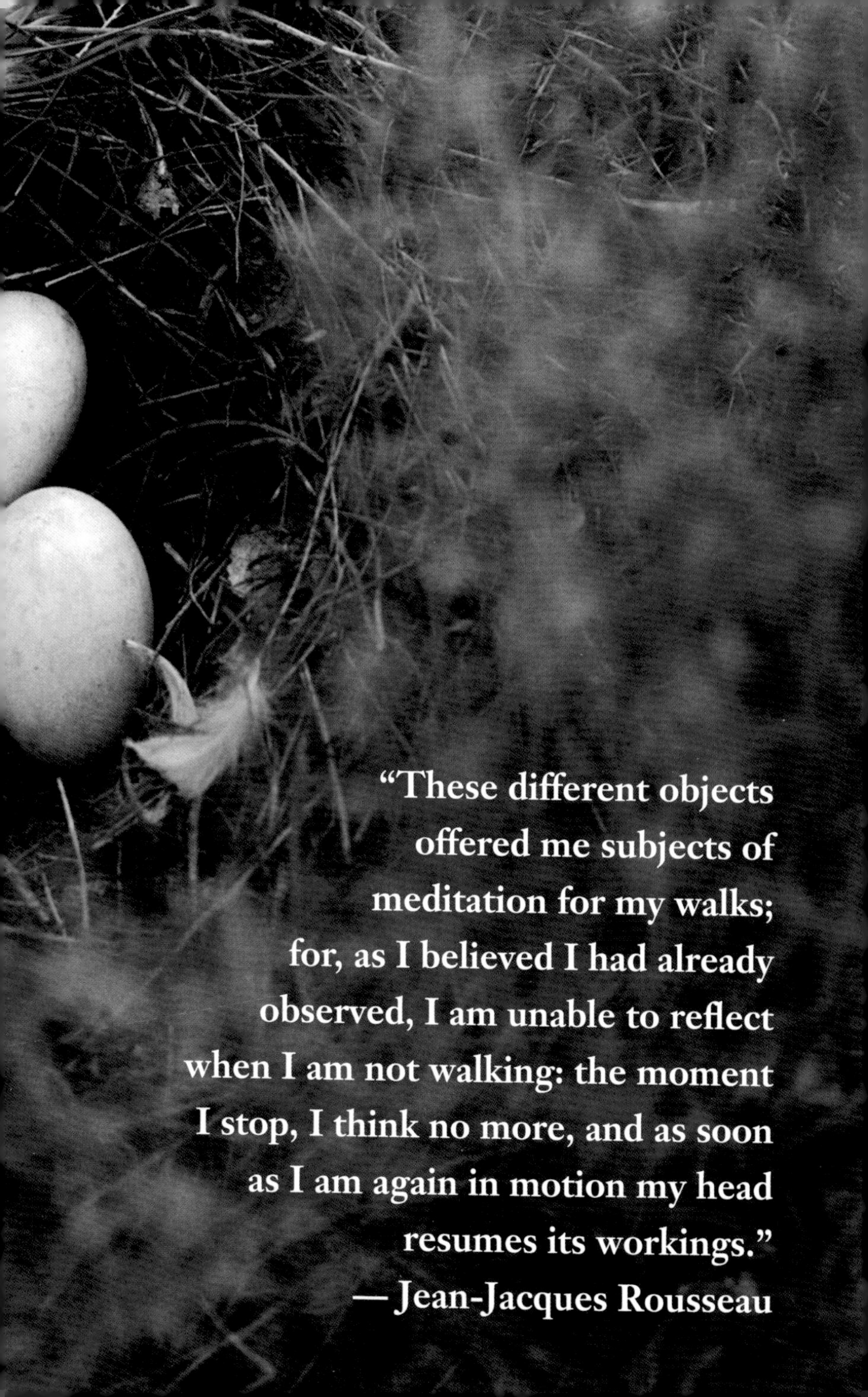
"These different objects
offered me subjects of
meditation for my walks;
for, as I believed I had already
observed, I am unable to reflect
when I am not walking: the moment
I stop, I think no more, and as soon
as I am again in motion my head
resumes its workings."
— Jean-Jacques Rousseau

Sense meditation involves the use of one or more senses to still the mind and create focus. For example, imagine stroking the soft fur of a cat or calm dog—in fact, do so if possible. Feel the softness between your fingertips. Let touch guide you, focusing only on the sensation of the nerve endings in your fingers. Forget all other senses for now. Only touch.

Be mindful of how your body responds. Where there is pain, meditate upon that part of the body. It's trying to alert you to something. Listen to your inner voice as it tells you what your pain is trying to say to you. Don't second-guess or rationalize it. The body speaks to you all the time. You must quiet the mind in order to listen.

Watching a bird soar in the blue sky, I feel my body begin to relax. My mind clears, thinking only of the flight of the bird. I imagine the wind lifting my body and the view of the earth below me. I sense the motion of soaring, diving, and climbing. My breathing slows, deep and steady, as I observe, detached from the rest of the world around me. I am one with the bird.

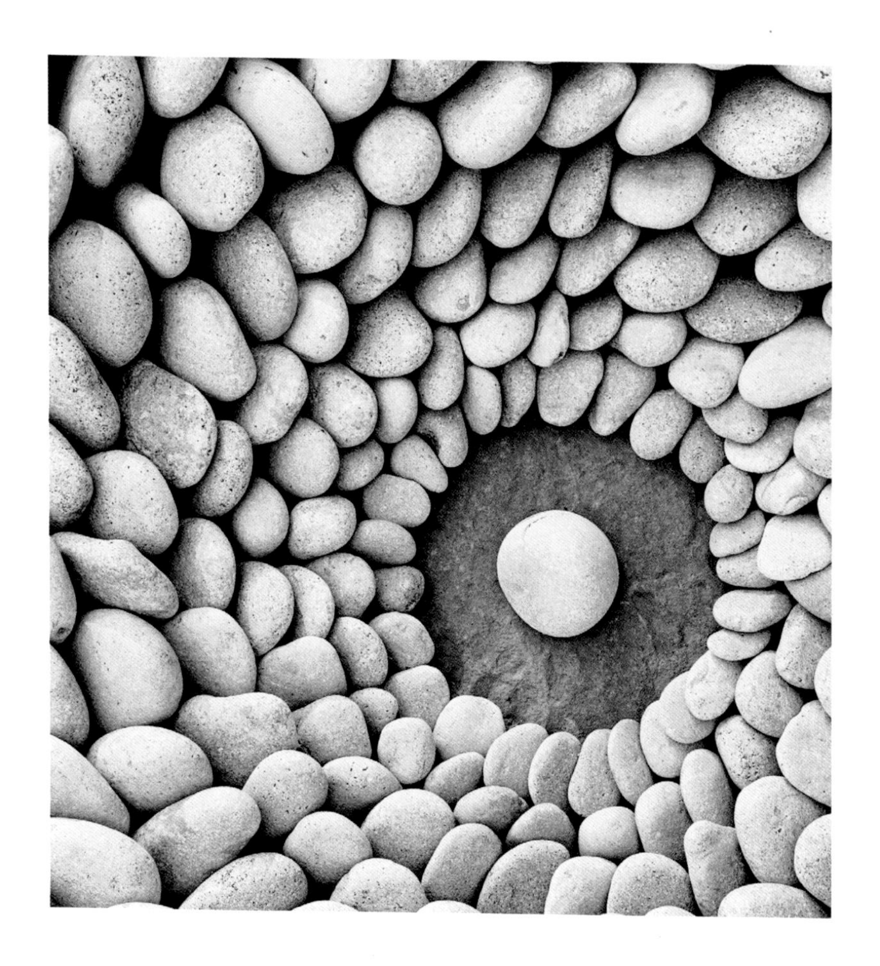

A mantra is a personal tool to help focus the mind and achieve a meditative state. It shouldn't become a crutch for the ability to become calm and still within. It simply symbolizes a direct path to that stillness—to where our spirit lives. The mantra is one of many roads that can lead us to a place of union with universal energy. It is not the only road.

Delores loved to swim, but rarely found the time with her busy work and family schedules. One hot summer day, she took a quick dip and found her body relaxing from the warm water. She swam slow laps, not rushing, in no hurry, letting her body stretch and enjoy the sensation of the water.

A half hour passed and she emerged feeling grounded and invigorated. The feeling carried her for the rest of the day, and Delores realized how much she needed to take time for herself each day. Swimming became her own meditation practice, and her body, mind, and spirit benefitted from it.

I am aware.
I am aware of my breath, giving me energy and vitality.
I am aware of my body, giving me motion and action.
I am aware of my thoughts, giving me ideas and goals.
I am aware of my spirit, giving me faith and inspiration.
I am aware of my soul, connection, and oneness.

I am one with the stillness within.
I am one with my surroundings. The universe speaks to me from this stillness. I am filled with light, peace, and healing. My intuition is sharpened and I am inspired. I am one with the force of the universe flowing through me. I am one with the stillness within.

Can meditation make you smarter? A UCLA research study found that people who meditate for years have higher levels of a process called "gyrification" which leads to faster processing in the brain's cortex region. The longer they meditated, the higher the levels of gyrification. Beginners or people who don't meditate have lower levels of this process.

Free the mind from clutter. Let thoughts drift off like clouds. Think only these things: Love, peace, joy. Become the essence of that thing with each breath, exhaling all else. Continue to breathe slowly and be with that one thought. Nothing else exists in this moment.

A preoccupied mind is not sharp or focused. Clearing out the clutter that muddles the mind is a great way to set and achieve new goals.

- Watch the thoughts you entertain and gravitate toward the positive ones.
- Catch yourself before you criticize something and instead choose acceptance.
- Begin each day with gratitude as your chosen attitude.
- Pause every few hours to breathe quietly for a minute.
- Stretch and make movement a part of your day.
- Fill your mind with visions of desired goals and how it feels to have them.

Love is pure being. I turn my mind to thoughts of love, becoming present to the energies of love that express in me and through me. Love surrounds me and I am immersed in it. In the moment, there is only love, no fear. Fear cannot withstand the power of love, and I am love in its human expression. My thoughts are of the love within me, the love around me, the love I am.

Being mindful means not judging anything to be good or bad—it means accepting experiences as they are. Being mindful means letting life flow through you instead of working against or in spite of you. It's a present-moment awareness that creates a sense of wellness and calm, where we operate from a place of unconditional love and acceptance. Being mindful means being present for life on its own terms, not ours.

Meditating on something painful or frightening can help dissipate its effects on the mind and body. Looking at something we fear loosens its grip on us, especially when we are in a calm, relaxed state of consciousness. Breathe into a problem and often the solution is what is exhaled. Focus on pain and, often, it begins to diminish.

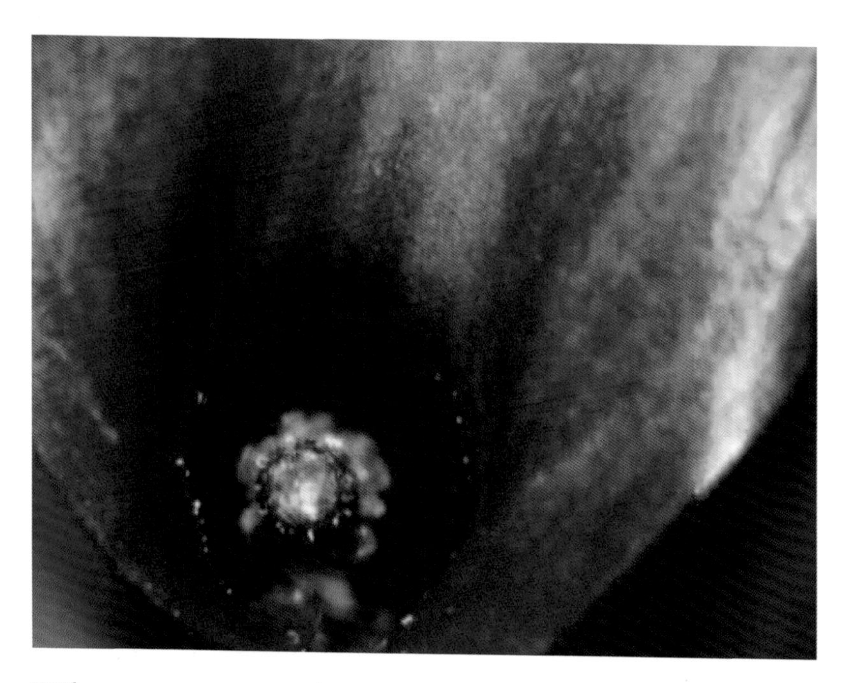

When my partner left me for someone else, I thought the heartbreak would be the end of me. I wanted to distract myself. I wanted to forget. But the mind has a way of insisting we face our demons, and I could no longer outrun mine. I meditated on the rejection, fear, and sadness I felt.

I focused more on my own inner spirit, and, in time, the pain became less noticeable. It didn't vanish overnight, but each day I was more able to find moments of happiness and laughter. Meditating brought me back to myself and the love I felt within.

Calming the mind and spirit, I focus my mind on patience. Here in the quiet of my inner world, I let go of expectations and timelines. I allow the present moment to unfold. I am mindful of each moment with no concerns for the future. I am patient, trusting, and relaxed. I am at peace.

Being mindful is good for you, but meditating mindfully is even better. Recent studies show that the brains of those who meditate have decreased sensitivity to pain, more dense gray matter in the brain stem, and other structural differences that improve cognitive, emotional, and immune responses. Meditation also leads to more emotional stability and mindful behavior.

Lydia spent two hours each day sitting in traffic. Her commute was making her crazy, and the stress was getting to her. Finally, she tried turning off the radio and accepting the situation. She used each hourlong trip to focus her mind and let negative energy slip away.

Lydia kept the radio off and her phone on silent. She used the time to breathe deeply and observe her surroundings. She made eye contact with other frustrated drivers and smiled. She felt more relaxed.

"You see what is happening all around us. The world is one of influence. Part of our energy is used up in the preservation of our own bodies. Beyond that, every particle of our energy is day and night being used in influencing others. Our bodies, our virtues, our intellect, and our spirituality, all these are continuously influencing others; and so, conversely, we are being influenced by them. This is going on all around us."

— Swami Vivekenanda

Can you find stillness anytime you want it?

Meditation practices lead to the empowering ability to become still and calm even amidst disaster and chaos. We learn to go within, breathing deeply, to find the center from which we can then face whatever challenges us from outside ourselves. The world around us can be upside-down but our mindfulness practice keeps us right-side-up.

Sit quietly and observe the marching of thoughts through your mind. Don't focus on any of them—only observe. See them as neutral, without emotion or power. Notice how many are positive and how many are critical or negative. Don't worry or become angry. Watch which thoughts demand to be noticed and which hide from conscious sight. Simply become aware of the thoughts that make up your reality. Then open your eyes and change what does not serve you.

If you want to reduce the cognitive decline that comes with aging, try what Buddhists have done for thousands of years. The integrity of gray matter is improved with meditation and has neuroprotective attributes that can help diminish age-related cognitive decline—something most people accept as an unavoidable part of aging.

Buddhist retreats teach meditation in the highest, purest form. But not many people can afford to take a few weeks off to attend one. Learning to meditate from a local organization served Lori just as well. She signed up for group lessons and began a practice of mindfulness that improved her health and introduced her to new friends.

Preparing your meditation space can itself be centering:

- Find the perfect spot indoors or outdoors with little noise or distraction.
- Pick a comfortable place to sit and a soft pillow.
- Use scented candles, scented oils, or herbs like sage to add the power of scent to your experience.
- Have a chosen mantra or object of focus ready for meditating upon.
- Breathe deeply in and out three times and begin your meditation.

I am formless. I am energy. I am light. I am vibration. I breathe in the energies of peace and harmony. I breathe out the energies of anger and fear. I become lighter with each breath, in and out, calming and expelling. I become free with each pass of air into my lungs, letting go of my burdens and cares. I am formless, boundless energy.

Acceptance is hard for many people. We want to control every aspect of our lives. Meditate on allowing life to be exactly as it is. Accept each experience as it unfolds, holding no resistance. Breathe into your center and be in the moment.

Shane's high-stress job left him little time for relaxing, and it was taking a toll. He was always on edge and often moody from the nonstop cortisol and adrenaline rush of work. Even at home, he felt "rushed." His friend Mark did yoga and meditation, and he was always so calm and positive.

Shane wasn't ready for yoga, but he tried meditation. He couldn't quiet his mind at first, but after a few dedicated attempts, he noticed he could detach from the noise of his brain. The feeling of serenity was amazing and carried over to his workday.

Pausing in the rushing and chaos of my day, I stop and breathe deeply. Closing my eyes, I bring my focus into the present, mindful of exactly where I am in this moment. Here, I rest for a while, just breathing. I am totally present and aware of my surroundings. My focus is laser sharp and my mind is clear. From this place of presence, I finish my day with clarity and calm.

Meditation that focuses on both internal and external stimuli can make you more creative. A Netherlands study showed that "open-monitoring" style meditation helped people perform better at tasks related to coming up with new ideas. Those who did more single focused meditation, as in focusing on the breath only, showed no improvement. Awareness is creative!

You may have a problem focusing on one thing or freeing the mind of thought. The essence of meditation is to let go with ease. Don't resist thoughts that intrude. Let them pass through the mind. Gently acknowledge them and consciously return focus to the task at hand. With practice, this will become easier and the mind will reach deeper levels of calm.

Everyone is different, but I never liked taking pharmaceuticals for my very high blood pressure. I always felt like they were a crutch, and that I needed to treat the problem, not the symptom. So I began eating healthier, lost some weight, and got my numbers down . . . But not enough.

I began a simple practice of 10-minute mindful meditation each morning and night. Only then did I see the big blood-pressure reduction I wanted—I slept better, lost more weight, and felt much less depressed and anxious. Wellness begins within.

Geri's daughter had a drug problem. It was devastating for her whole family but especially to Geri—she felt had failed as a mother. She couldn't fix or control the situation. Geri knew she had to take care of herself or she wouldn't be able to hold her family together.

She began to spend quiet time, breathing, focusing only on the present moment and the respite it offered from her pain. Geri realized she could get through anything if she just focused on the moment at hand. Meditation became a way for her to restore calm and perspective.

The spirit within me recognizes the spirit in all things. From deep within my center, my spirit moves, embracing all that this moment holds. I sense the true essence of others and acknowledge their divinity. I express my own uniqueness and allow others the expression of theirs. In my meditation, my mind is silent, and my spirit speaks clearly, guiding and directing my path.

"Meditation means the mind is turned back upon itself. The mind stops and the world stops. Your consciousness expands. Every time you meditate you will keep your growth. Work a little harder, more and more, and meditation comes. You do not feel the body or anything else. When you come out of it after the hour, you have had the most beautiful rest you ever had in your life."

— Swami Vivekenanda

Teaching my restless son to meditate helped him with anxiety issues in school. I began with a short few minutes of simply being aware of his breathing, something he could do anywhere, even in class. He began to report less anxiety as he learned to alleviate and redirect his nervous self-talk.

Now he has a powerful tool to help him stay calm, and his state of mind and grades have improved. He even told a couple of his friends and showed them how to "belly breathe" when they have a test or a bad day. Mindfulness should be taught in all schools.

With the overwhelming amount of information bombarding our brains today, it's hard to stay focused. Distractions are everywhere! But a 2012 American study showed that mindfulness-based meditation worked wonders at decreasing stress, allowing the subjects to multitask better than those who didn't meditate.

Meditation can be done anytime and anywhere you can squeeze in a bit of solitude during your busy daily life. Look for a quiet place with no interruptions and power off or silence your cell phone. Get comfortable and find a place to sit if you can. Now, just breathe. Do this for at least five minutes, and you'll feel rejuvenated for the rest of the day.

I am the universe poured into one small vessel. I breathe and turn within, feeling a connection to the web of life: I am a strand in that web and a vital portion of the whole web. I release my notions of being alone, lonely, and separate. I am a piece of the whole and the whole itself. I am the universe in microcosm. I am the universe in human form.

Regular meditation impacts more than the brain's physical and chemical structures. In fact, neurologists have found decreased activity in the brain functions responsible for lapses of attention, anxiety disorders, and ADHD. Meditation is good medicine!

Janine couldn't forgive the parent who had abused her as a child. Abuse haunted her into adulthood, fostering depression and a fear of abandonment. Her relationships suffered and her health did, too. She took a class on mindfulness and one night the topic was forgiveness. They meditated on it. Janine resisted—how could she clear her mind of so much pain?

But soon she found herself releasing the anger and hurt. With each new meditation, she found more strength to forgive her father and to forgive herself for holding the resentment for so long. She felt a huge weight lift off her shoulders.

Meditation can help lessen pain. Focusing on the breath, or a mantra, helps keep the mind occupied and the body relaxed. Imagine white, healing light moving over the painful area. Feel it permeate every cell of the body. Breathe into the pain and embrace the light, then breathe out the pain, letting only light remain.

Energy is life. During meditation, imagine you are nothing but vibrating waves of energy. Visualize your vibration rising higher. Give it a light and vivid color and a positive sensation. Experience the life energy moving through your body, lifting each cell into a vibration of healing and wholeness. Let your heart match the frequency of joy.

Notice a flower in bloom as you go about your day, or picture one in your mind. Look closely at the intricacy of the petals. Imagine scents that soothe the mind and delight the soul. Remember peaceful walks in parks and gardens. We are nourished by the sun's warm rays. We raise our faces toward the sky.

One of the most profound days of my life involved a deep meditation. I was depressed, unable to find a job, and mentally and emotionally exhausted. I sat quietly in my bedroom listening to the sound of cars going by on the street outside. I closed my eyes, and soon was deep into meditation.

Awareness of my physical body slipped away, and I was formless. I was one with the cars rushing by outside, and one with the floor beneath me. I felt all solid matter turn to pure vibration, and dwelled in the energy of my being. When I awoke, I felt like I'd slept for weeks. Refreshed, renewed, and with new hope.

Senses resonating with sounds and smells
Colors clearer, brighter, alive, and intense
Ego dissipates—only consciousness remains
Awareness of self as part of all there is
Floating on a higher plane, fully awakened
Spirit soars, leaving the weight of the body behind

Heart disease is a major cause of death. But a 2012 study of people with coronary disease showed that taking a class in transcendental meditation reduced their risk of heart disease, stroke, and death by 48%. People who meditate have long said their practice keeps them healthy. Studies like this offer evidence of the powerful link between mind and body.

Vital energy flows through me as I sit in stillness. My mind calms and I am in tune with the vibration of the energy within. I let this energy expand outward, creating an aura of abundance, joy, and happiness that affects those I come in contact with. I am vibrant with the life force. I radiate rays of love.

Larry couldn't sit still. He knew the benefits of meditation from his wife, who combined it with a yoga practice, but yoga wasn't for him. He loved to hike, and decided to combine his passion for hiking with his desire to lead a more mindful, centered life. It was hard to focus on anything while physically exerting himself, and he realized the exertion was calming.

His meditation practice became the great outdoors, and how his body and mind aligned as he hiked a dirt trail. He looked forward to it and noticed the benefits to his physical and emotional health.

"There is something servile in the habit of seeking after a law which we may obey. We may study the laws of matter at and for our convenience, but a successful life knows no law. It is an unfortunate discovery certainly, that of a law which binds us where we did not know before that we were bound. Live free, child of the mist—and with respect to knowledge we are all children of the mist."

— Henry David Thoreau

Visualize a beautiful beach. The air is warm, the sand white and clean. Listen to the rush of the waves and the call of gulls flying overhead. Children laugh as they run past. Feel the sun's rays on your skin. Taste sea salt upon your lips as time slows down. The cool breeze rustles your hair. You are relaxed, completely at peace.

Mindful meditation is not about a mind empty of thought so much as a mind that is not bound by thought: a mind that can allow thought to enter and exit without judgment or resistance; a mind that is clear enough to choose thoughts and discard others; a mind that is full of the present moment, and the thoughts that reside there, but not beholden to those thoughts.

"This external world is only the world of suggestion. A grain of sand gets washed into the shell of an oyster and irritates it. The irritation produces a secretion in the oyster, which covers the grain of sand and the beautiful pearl is the result. Similarly, external things furnish us with suggestions, over which we project our own ideals and make our objects."

— Swami Vivekenanda

Music is a wonderful way to help free the mind from worries. Meditate on a concerto or other piece of classical music, and let the **left brain** take a back seat as the **right brain** opens to creativity and inspiration. Music meditation is about lifting the spirit, not about the song itself, so choose what moves you without fear of judgment. Consciousness shifts and the mind is expanded and awakened.

So much of life draws our attention outward—my life was filled with stress and I was on autopilot. I enjoyed my activities less and less, until I sat on my bed one day and went quiet. With no TV or phone or distractions, I was able to turn inward.

In a few minutes, I felt a stunning calm seep into my mind. I began to relax into my breathing, not worried about what I needed to do or "should" be thinking about. I felt present and wished to keep that sensation forever. But I'm able to return daily to calm myself.

Close your eyes and listen. We focus so much on the visual that we often forget the power of sound. Natural sounds all around us calm and soothe the spirit. People talking and laughing make us feel less alone and isolated. The wind in the treetops lulls us into a relaxed state. Our breath and heartbeat remind us we are vibrantly, joyfully alive.

Music is the language of the soul. Let the melody of a favorite song lift your spirit as you allow your body to sink into relaxation. Become the notes. Feel the deep bass, the fairy wings of delicate staccatos. Become one with the music and feel your form melt away. Allow the notes to resonate through every part of your being. Let your spirit dance.

Quietly move your focus into your deepest mind. Visualize white light rising through the base of your body, healing and empowering each part as it moves upward toward the crown of your head. Let the light leave the crown and expand outward, creating an aura around you of healing and protection.

Allow the mind to drift with no end goal. Let thoughts be as they ebb and flow with no expectation. Breathe in and out, observing but not reacting. Let everything happen without necessity of control. The mind drifts. Thoughts move like waves on the sand. Breath comes and goes. Life is in this moment, here and now.

Our greatest ideas come to us in silence and solitude, where the whisper of intuition can only be discerned above the shout of intellect and the raucousness of reason. When we fill our days with the noisy blur of constant activity, we miss the gifts and blessings of silence and stillness. Silence is more than golden. It's essential to a life well lived.

Become present to the ways spiritual energy works in your life. It's hard to see or feel spirit when we are so distracted. Mindfulness is returning to spirit to communicate, learn, and grow. Only in the now can we hear the voice of our own spirit calling, and we must become quiet and still in order to hear it.

I spent most of my life either planning for my future or stressing out over my past, until I realized how much time I was wasting. Mindfulness taught me to get back to the present and to become mindful of what I was doing each moment of the day. It taught me to tune in to my body and world in a way I rarely had before.

"We seldom break our leg so long as life continues a toilsome upward climb. The danger comes when we begin to take things easily and choose the convenient paths."

— Friedrich Nietzsche

Mindfulness meditation trains the mind to let go of thoughts that lead to stress in the body. Meditation leads to calmness and serenity that are healing and powerful, and meditation brings balance to chaotic lives. Holding onto thoughts that don't serve us is taxing and tiring. Being mindful allows us to surrender to what does serve us.

Many of us don't breathe deeply enough. Be mindful of your breath and how much air you bring in. Breathe into the belly, not the chest, for the greatest benefit. Put your hand on your belly and feel it rise with each inhale. If it isn't rising, you're depriving your body of precious energy.

Mindfulness means:

- Staying focused on the task at hand.
- Noticing everything as it comes into your experience.
- Acknowledging and accepting the present situation.
- Living in the moment and having goals for the future.
- Operating from a calm center that's grounded in love.
- Keeping an open mind.

Wherever you are, be there wholly. Be present and awake to what is. Stop wanting to be somewhere else. You are here. Stop wanting to be something else. You are this. Stay on your breath as you experience the sense of authentic living that comes from being here and being you.

"A man's ignorance sometimes is not only useful, but beautiful—while his knowledge, so called, is oftentimes worse than useless, besides being ugly. Which is the best man to deal with—he who knows nothing about a subject, and, what is extremely rare, knows that he knows nothing, or he who really knows something about it, but thinks that he knows all?"

— Henry David Thoreau

Today I feel alone, yet I am not lonely. There is peace in solitude and rejuvenation in the quiet of being alone. I lead my thoughts to restful healing. I use this time alone to find myself and reach deep inside my heart and mind to find peace. I rejoice in being away from the noise and clatter of everyday life.

This long, loud, and noisy day threatens to overwhelm me, and there are still so many hours to go before I sleep. Will it ever end? Will I ever know the precious sound of golden silence? Even in the chaos, I close my eyes and picture a clearing in the woods with a cold, clear stream running through it. Reflection helps to ground me and put my challenges in perspective.

Shawn's boss was a narcissist with little compassion for his employees. Shawn worked late every night and went home feeling sick, only to have to get up and do it all over again the next day. He had always meditated for guidance but did so now more than ever.

In the calm of his mindfulness practice, Shawn realized he had options, even if the unknown was scary. He centered himself enough to find the courage to quit his job and start his own company, something he never could have done without first finding his inner strength.

As I breathe deeply, time slows down to a singular moment—the now. I relax here, sensing with a greater awareness the timelessness of experience. Spirit within knows no boundaries of time. I am spirit. I am without boundaries of time. The now I rest in is eternal, with no beginning or end. In the now, I am forever.

Dim the lights in a quiet room and light a candle. Watch the flame and let thoughts drift away as your mind focuses on the dance of light. Drop your shoulders and let your eyelids droop, allowing the flame to hypnotize and relax you. Breathe in through your nose and out through your mouth. Become the dancing flame as your sensation of having a body dissipates. Become the light in the darkness.

Meditate on a cup of warm tea. Hold the mug, feeling the heat against your palms. Lift the cup and smell the aroma of the tea rising in wisps through the air. Taste the tea, letting your mouth delight in the experience. Savor the entire cup, staying mindful and focused on the tea and how it makes you feel.

Doing a meditation isn't about becoming a yogi or guru—it's about improving your health. Even sitting quietly for five minutes is better than nothing at all. Sometimes we let the pressure to do well prevent us from trying new things, but mindfulness is about understanding our limits and accepting them! Try meditating, and soon you'll find your groove.

I am breath. I am energy. I am light. I am the force of life itself within my body, expressing outward into my world. I am the flow and process of life, moving in rhythm with every heartbeat. I am consciousness made manifest. With each breath, I am immersed in this vibrant, creative, and empowering energy of love.

"He is bound by a thousand chains which press on him so as to leave no moment free. And perhaps it seems to him that, were he free, he should but feel the more forlorn. It is an element to which his mental frame has not been trained. He knows not what to do to-day or to-morrow; how to stay by himself, or how to meet others; how to act, or how to rest."

— Margaret Fuller

Human beings are the only creatures that strive to be something they are not. Perhaps we should take a lesson from the birds of the sky, who never ache to be anything other than creatures able to fly on a lifting breeze. Or learn from the fish of the sea, who don't doubt their own ability to glide through blue waters dappled with sunlight. Or spend some time watching wild horses thunder over the open plains, and we would see that not once do they stop to wish they were anything more than glorious, beautiful, and free.

“There is no help for you outside of yourself; you are the creator of the universe. Like the silkworm you have built a cocoon around yourself. Burst your own cocoon and come out as the beautiful butterfly, as the free soul. Then alone you will see Truth.”

— Swami Vivekenanda

Just before sunrise, I sit in my meditation area and travel inward. I spend time totally present to life, with no sense of being hurried. As the sun comes up, I focus my mind on the light and colors, watching as the life-giving star rises higher in the sky. I breathe in sunlight, invigorating my bloodstream. I am ready for the day.

"Meditation supplied the want of knowledge, and a very natural reflection gave strength to my resolutions, which was, that whether I lived or died, I had no time to lose."

—Jean-Jacques Rousseau

Something happens that derails our plans. We react. Mindfulness teaches us to become aware of our own thoughts and actions so that we don't have kneejerk responses to life. Instead, we learn to get into the present moment and choose the best response from a position of awareness, wisdom, and power. We become responsible, not reactive.

Being mindful requires nothing. Be quiet and present. Be awake and aware. Don't work on removing thought—let thought be. Don't worry about how the body feels—let the body be. Focus on everything and nothing, freeing the mind to do as it will. Allow everything to simply be, without struggle or effort.

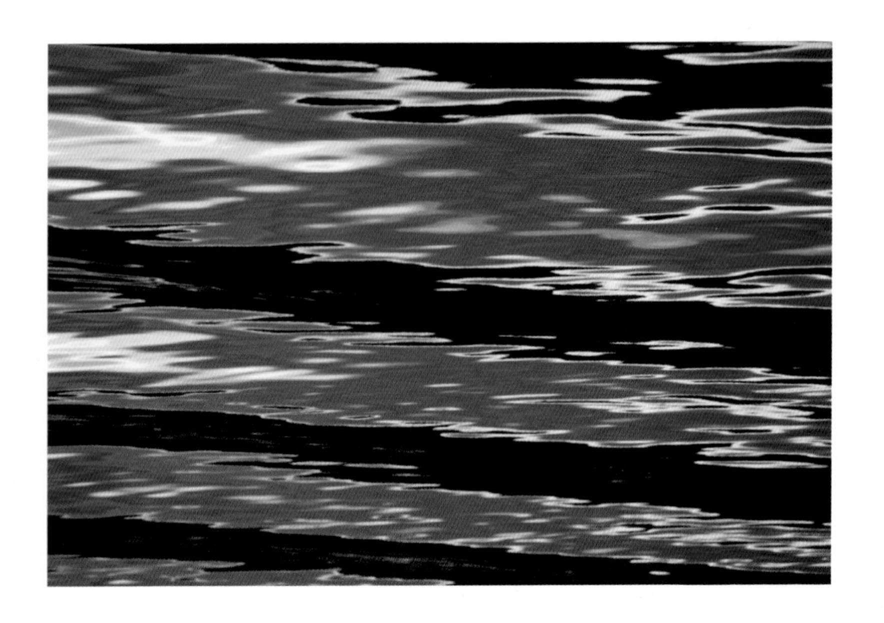

Max was facing back surgery. He had insurance but wanted to minimize his time away from work—he was falling behind and could be replaced. After surgery, he had medication to help him get through, but it was his mindfulness meditation that really sped up his recovery.

Max meditated twice daily, focusing on the present and using a mantra for healing that he created himself. He did a unique breathing pattern taught to him by a yoga teacher, and soon he felt his pain lessening and moving to the periphery of his mind. Meditation didn't cure the pain, but it did help him cope and move past it until his body healed itself.

When we fill our days with the noisy blur of constant activity, we miss the gifts and blessings of silence and stillness. Only by purposely taking the time to do nothing can we cultivate the inner wisdom and calm we seek. It's in the quiet that we renew our connection to the source of inspiration, energy, and enthusiasm.

"I love to amuse myself by beginning a hundred things, by following a fly through all its windings, in wishing to overturn a rock to see what is under it; finally, in musing from morning until night without order or coherence, and in following in everything the caprice of a moment."

—Jean-Jacques Rousseau

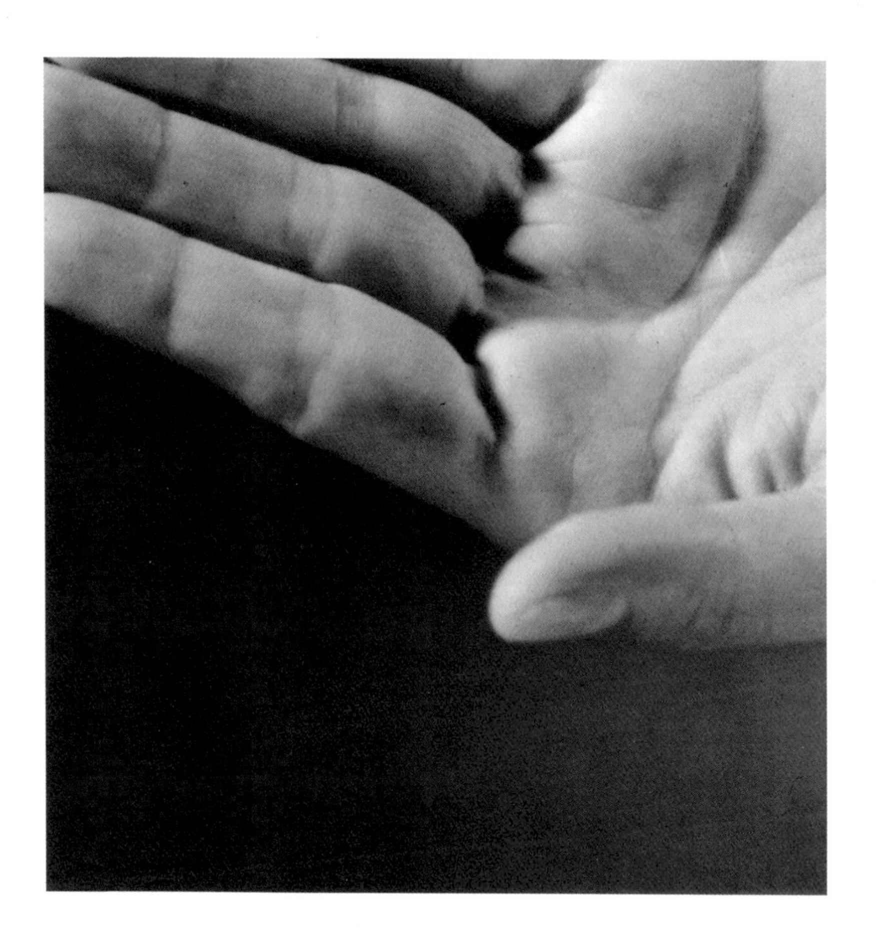

Pick up an object in the room and focus your attention on it. Feel it in your hands. Is it smooth or rough? Cool or warm? Does it have a scent? Look closely at the materials. Hold it up to the light and examine it. Focus only on this object. This exercise teaches you to see something instead of merely looking at it.

In your mind exists a door. Visualize this door opening. Go through the door into a beautiful place vibrant with light and color. There is a wise person waiting. Sit with this person in silence, absorbing their unspoken guidance. When you feel ready, go back through the door, carrying with you the wisdom of your inner spirit.

When my final grandparent died, I took time to turn within and allow my mind to think deeply about what death meant. In the stillness, fears and doubts emerged, gripping me with their force. But soon I felt the fear and doubt begin to move away, replaced by an overwhelming calm.

In my meditation, I've come to fear death less as a final ending. In the center of my being is a place where I no longer exist as a body but instead as pure spirit.

I quiet my mind and enter the flow of life within me and around me. I am present to this flow. I am this flow. I allow and accept where the river of life takes me. I remain centered and at peace. As life asks me to bend, I bend. As life asks me to move, I move. As life asks me to be, I am still. I am open to life as it comes to me.

Sit with anger or fear that you may feel. Relax your body and calm your mind and see anger and fear as nothing but energy in the body. Allow this energy to move and express, then visualize it leaving the body and dissipating. Fill your body with healing energy, peace, and faith. Sit with this new energy.

"To be for once entirely powerless! the plaything of the elementary forces of nature! There is a restfulness in this happiness, a casting away of the great burden, a descent without fatigue, as if one had been given up to the blind force of gravity."

— Friedrich Nietzsche

Today belongs to you. It's a clean page you can cover with wonderful, creative images and words that will fill every moment with satisfaction. In moments of awe and wonder, we become re-enchanted with the magic of our everyday lives—magic that is ever-present, but often overlooked.

Take time to reflect on the people and things around you. It is in these quiet moments that inspiration grows and we recognize the miracle of life. No day should ever be so hectic that there is not time in it for solitude and reflection.

I am here. I begin breathing, inhaling and holding the breath for five beats. I am here. I exhale slowly, feeling the air move out of my lungs. I am here. I inhale again, filling my body with life-giving air. I am here. I exhale, to a count of five, letting go of stress. I am here. I breathe in, I breathe out. I am here.

"The soul of man is like a piece of crystal, but it takes the colour of whatever is near it. Suppose a red flower is near the crystal and the crystal takes the colour and forgets itself, thinks it is red. This is the ordinary person. It is the person taking the colour of the flower near to it. We are no more bodies than the crystal is the red flower."

— Swami Vivekananda

Feeling lost and unanchored should remind us to get back to our center. In mindful meditation, we breathe ourselves toward a pure state of spirit. Doing this every day keeps us authentic and grounded, operating from our own personal integrity, truth, and power.

As my mind calms, I begin to feel a serenity deep within. I settle into this feeling, immersed in the peace it brings. Nothing can bring me fear in this place. Nothing can harm me in the stillness of my mind. I am totally aware of the present, and nothing of the past or future can affect me here.

Erika loved managing a seaside gift shop, but there were times she wanted to cry from the needy crowds and her uncaring boss. So she started taking "meditation breaks." She'd excuse herself and sit in the back room for a few minutes, closing her eyes and breathing deeply from her belly, feeling grounded and re-energized.

Soon, her employees noticed how calm she was and began taking mediation breaks of their own. The store felt calmer even in the crush of tourist season.

Be still and listen to the whisper of your intuition within. Let it speak to you with the guidance and wisdom you seek. Relax the body, rest the intellect, and quiet the mind—allow your heart to have its voice. Be still in this loving and safe place, and know that you are precious, unique, and important.

"The less passion there is, the better we work. The calmer we are, the better for us and the more the amount of work we can do. When we let loose our feelings, we waste so much energy, shatter our nerves, disturb our minds, and accomplish very little work."

— Swami Vivekananda

We live in a society that knows nothing of delayed gratification; we get caught up in the expectation that everything we need and ask for will happen immediately. But we must be grateful, we must be mindful of the bounty we have, and we must find our important lessons inside ourselves. We are blessed and privileged to have time for reflection and growth.

Much of mindfulness training involves silencing and setting aside our smartphones, but there are many meditation apps that can help you structure your mindfulness practice. If you carry guided meditations in your pocket, you'll be surprised by how many new opportunities you'll find in your day.

"Everything has its wonders,
even darkness and silence,
and I learn,
whatever state I may be in,
therein to be content."

— Helen Keller

Freedom comes from forgiveness. I quiet my thoughts and let go of resentful ones. I visualize anger and regret—they move further from me with each exhale of breath. In the now I am able to let go and forgive. The past is gone. There is only this moment and I am free from past mistakes and burdens. I forgive and move on.

I am not my pain and suffering.
I am not my thoughts and behaviors.
I am not the shape or size of my body parts.
I am not my job or position in life.
I am not my goals and achievements.
I am not how much money I make.
I am not the things I own.
I am not what I do or what I don't do.
I am none of these things—
And I am all of these things.

Be present with this experience. Do not let time rush you. Breathe and simply be in the here and now. Do not let time concern you. Pay attention. Do not let time worry you. Flow with life without resistance. Do not let time frighten you. Live for each moment. Do not let time hurry you.

“Our imagination is higher when our stomach is not overloaded; in spring than in winter; in solitude than amidst company; and in an obscured light than in the blaze and heat of the noon.”

— Isaac Disraeli

"We must overcome difficulty by constant practice. We must learn that nothing can happen to us unless we make ourselves susceptible to it."

— Swami Vivekananda

Finding my center, I radiate peace.
Finding my soul, I radiate light.
Finding my spirit, I radiate joy.
Finding my heart, I radiate love.
Grounded in spirit, I express my essence.
Grounded in earth, I embrace my humanity.
Grounded in life, I am a unique spark.
Grounded in the now, I am timeless.

What is bliss but to be in the moment? I release the worries of the day and sink into a blissful state, available to the flow of life. I am a walking meditation, breathing and moving with calm purpose. I allow myself to feel my feelings, not reject them. I feel connected, empowered, and happy where I am.

Guidance from within only comes to us when we are quiet enough to hear it. If you have a question in need of an answer, be quiet and present, and listen to your mind. Don't force anything to come to you, but be ready to hear what does come.

Set your mind free of constraints. Be in the moment where all possibility exists. Feel the joy of the freedom when the sky is your only limit. As you breathe, inhale pure potential. As you breathe, focus on intention. Here in the mind, all dreams go from invisible to manifest. Breathe in the dream, breathe out the form.

Light is energy. I breathe in light and energize my body, mind, and spirit. The light washes over every part of me that is tired, rejuvenating and refreshing it with pure and joyful enthusiasm. I envision the light surrounding my body like an aura of good vibrations. My mind is clear and focused. I am ready.

Parents can teach their children mindfulness as a way to cope with and reduce school stress. It's never too early to show children the power of the present moment and mindful breathing. They can become more aware of life around them and more compassionate to others and themselves.

"What a morning that was! Every sight is worth twice as much by the early morning light. We borrow something of the spirit of the hour to look upon them."

— Margaret Fuller

The earth is asleep. The buds of spring lie in wait. The wonder of the world seems in a holding pattern, waiting for the go-ahead to grow. Let winter teach you the value of stillness, of silence, and of meditation. Nature's quiet time of regeneration may spark the same in you.

There is no resistance in the present. I breathe in and out, knowing only this moment of my experience. I am free of the obstacles of past and future, free of worry and regret. I exist only now and as pure energy. I am free from judgment and opinion. I am free from boundaries and separation. In the present, I am one with the consciousness of all.

Carrie worked in social services for ten years, and the people she dealt with and the suffering she saw were getting to her. She was always tired and got sick easily. She knew she had to find ways to alleviate stress if she wanted to continue the work she loved, so she took up mindfulness meditation and practiced yoga three times a week.

Soon she was able to address the suffering of her many clients with more love, compassion, and strength. Taking care of her own body and mind allowed her to be more present for others, and she rediscovered the joy and satisfaction of her calling.

I watch thoughts drift by like debris on ocean waves. In the stillness of my spirit, I am the observer. I don't hold onto things or let go of things. I let them float past. I feel no need to own or demand. I have no goals or motivations. In the stillness of my spirit, I am everything and anything I need already. I am complete and whole and free.

In this moment, I have no needs or desires. My mind is at peace, letting all thoughts flow loosely without attachment to outcome. I breathe and pay attention to the movement of air in my lungs. My senses are sharp and aware, merging into a sense of unity with my surroundings. I have no needs or demands for this moment. I am simply here.

"Let us say that here is an infinite line amid darkness. We do not see the line, but on it there is one luminous point which moves on. As it moves along the line, it lights up its different parts in succession, and all that is left behind becomes dark again. Our consciousness may be likened to this luminous point. Its past experiences have been replaced by the present, or have become subconscious. We are not aware of their presence in us; but there they are, unconsciously influencing our body and mind."

— Swami Vivekananda

Your mind is a powerful tool for healing.

- Do not allow illness to consume your identity.
- Focus your thoughts on wholeness and wellness.
- Breathe into pain and let it move through you.
- Stay present to keep worry and fear at arm's length.
- Visualize your body and spirit as well and whole.

I meditate upon death and open my mind to the essence of the experience. Death is a transition of energy. Without my body, I am pure formless energy that can't be destroyed. In death, my energy shifts and takes a new form. Death is not an end, but another beginning. Acceptance helps me feel at peace.

Love is a powerful force. Calm the mind and allow love to flow through you, bringing light to dark corners of your mind and your soul. Allow love to be the focus as you breathe. Relax into love and feel it encompass your entire body. Visualize love moving through you and outward into the world. Meditate on love and become love.

"There is the external universe and universal spirit, mind, ether, gas, luminosity, liquid, solid. The same with the mind. I am just exactly the same in the microcosm. I am the spirit; I am mind; I am the ether, solid, liquid, gas. What I want to do is to go back to my spiritual state. It is for the individual to live the life of the universe in one short life."

— Swami Vivekananda

Exercise can be meditative. Focus on your muscles as they contract and relax. Feel the building sense of effort and fatigue with each repetition. Let the routine quiet your mind as you practice motions again and again. The body and mind work together as one.

I never understood the power of breath until I began a meditation practice. I chose to use a mantra, and found I could chant in rhythm with my breath, producing a powerful sensation of calm and awareness. My senses came alive as I heard sounds and smelled scents so much more clearly.

Even outside of meditation, I learned to breathe more deeply and effectively, a priceless exercise for whenever life gets to be too hectic. It grounds me in the present moment and brings me back to a state of mindfulness.

You are not alone. Breathe into the connection with life around you. Feel your ego and boundaries melt away as union with all of nature fills you with peace. Stay in this peace, fully present, aware of your self but a part of the greater whole. With each breath, you are merging into that energy. You are not alone.

Be mindful of a rainy day and let your stress slip away. Listen to the falling rain and lose yourself in the patter on the window. Breathe deeply the smell of nourished soil. Let your worry wash away with the rain, leaving your mind cleansed. Sit with the sights, sounds, and smells of rainfall and allow them to renew and refresh your spirit.

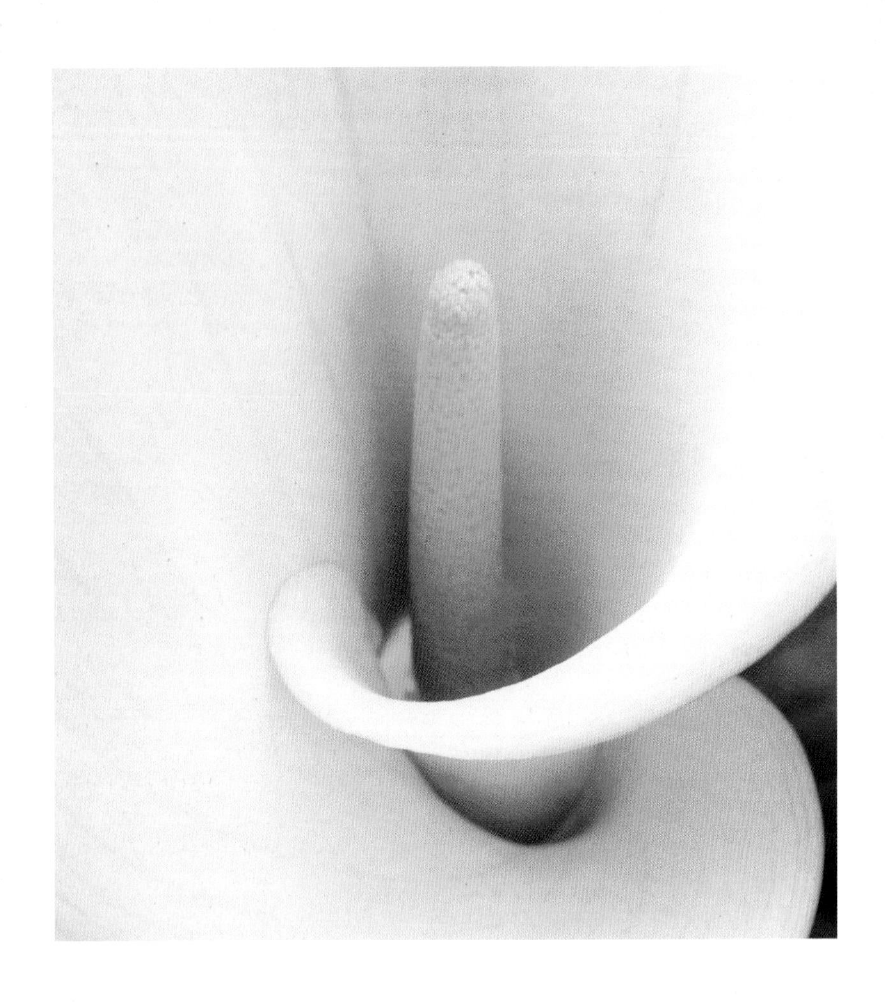

“When you think of yourself as a body, you forget that you are a mind, and when you think of yourself as a mind, you will forget the body. There is only one thing, that you are; you can see it either as matter or body — or you can see it as mind or spirit.”

— Swami Vivekananda

In the solitude of a natural setting, the heart discovers serenity, the soul knows abiding peace, and the spirit finds renewal. Surround yourself with the serenity of nature, and you will feel more at peace with yourself and your world.

I am not living my life—my life is living me. I turn within to the stillness and feel the source of life stirring up, desiring expression through me. I am aware and mindful of my connection to this source, and I let it move without restriction. I am living mindfully, authentically, and joyfully.

Set a timer for ten minutes, get comfortable, and sit quietly. Let your eyelids droop and close, let your breathing deepen, and expect nothing. Gently move thoughts through your mind, holding onto none. Have no goal or purpose except to be present to the world around you and within you.

"I have met with but one or two persons in the course of my life who understood the art of Walking, that is, of taking walks—who had a genius, so to speak, for sauntering. For this is the secret of successful sauntering. He who sits still in a house all the time may be the greatest vagrant of all; but the saunterer, in the good sense, is no more vagrant than the meandering river, which is all the while sedulously seeking the shortest course to the sea."

— Henry David Thoreau

I chant my mantra slowly and softly, letting the sound of my voice carry my thoughts away. Focused on the power of my mantra, I feel my body disappear as I become pure spirit, pure consciousness. The vibration of the words resonates in the frequencies of love, peace, and harmony. I chant my mantra and I am at peace.

Sandra answers phones all day and often feels frazzled and overwhelmed. Customers take their frustrations out on her, though she knows they don't mean to; but knowing she isn't a "real person" to them doesn't help, either.

One day a coworker asked if Sandra could cover his calls for a few minutes while things were slow. It turns out he takes a short break each day to breathe rhythmically and restore a feeling of balance and intention. Sandra agreed to trade off so she can take a break, too. She breathes in for a count of five and breathes out very slowly, sometimes stretching if she's extra tense.

"Go forward with courage. When you are in doubt be still and wait; when doubt no longer exists for you, then go forward with courage. So long as mists envelope you, be still; be still until the sunlight pours through and dispels the mists—as it surely will. Then act with courage."

— White Eagle

"The greatest help to spiritual life is meditation. In meditation we divest ourselves of all material conditions and feel our divine nature. We do not depend upon any external help in meditation. The touch of the soul can paint the brightest colour even in the dingiest places; it can cast a fragrance over the vilest thing; it can make the wicked divine."

— Swami Vivekananda

You are made of golden sun and silver starlight. You are one with the universe, no separation of space and time. You are whirling galaxy and red dwarf star. You are the darkness in between matter and the light of distant worlds. You are the cosmos and the quantum, the grand and the miniscule.

In the midst of emotional suffering I find a place of peace. I go within, focusing my thoughts only on my breath and the moment at hand. I sink into the feelings of pain and loss, letting them be what they are without judgment. They move through me without resistance or blockage. I process them from a deep place of inner strength.

Slow the pace of your life and your thoughts. Life is not a race. Sit quietly for a few moments, paying attention to what your mind is doing. Free it from worry, fear, and to-do lists, and let it wander where it wants to go. Sense the deeper mind beneath, and go there. Here, there is peace and beauty. Here, there are no lists or clocks. Dwell here for a while.

The next time you sit down to eat, don't rush the process. Pay attention to each bite of food. Meditate on the taste, the smell, and the texture of what you are eating. Food is energy and nourishment. Food keeps us alive. Feel your body respond to the pleasure of eating. Be present to the meal and enjoy and savor every bite.

"Everywhere and at all times it is in thy power piously to acquiesce in thy present condition, and to behave justly to those who are about thee, and to exert thy skill upon thy present thoughts, that nothing shall steal into them without being well examined."

— Marcus Aurelius

Recognize that not all being alone is loneliness, and not all solitude is a problem to solve. Rejoice in discovering the blessings of quietness. Seek comfort in the garden, seek adventure in the wilderness, seek laughter in companionship, but seek the truth within yourself.

Awaken to the present and the timeless movement of life. Let the mind become aware of the landscape of past, present, and future as one. In the singular moment, there is nothing but the moment. Be immersed where there is no space and time.

"The art of meditation may be exercised at all hours, and in all places; and men of genius, in their walks, at table, and amidst assemblies, turning the eye of the mind inwards, can form an artificial solitude; retired amidst a crowd, calm amidst distraction, and wise amidst folly."

— Isaac Disraeli

Meditation always seemed impossible to me until a friend suggested running meditation. I tried it the next day on my long run along the beach. I let the movement of air in and out of my lungs be my focus. I tuned in to the sound of my breath, yet I was totally aware of my surroundings.

The longer I ran, the more my senses came alive. I felt one with the people passing me, the ocean waves rolling onto the sand, the noisy gulls overhead. I'd lost focus on my breathing and was a part of everything around me. My daily runs have become my meditation practice. Stillness and quietude don't require sitting still.

"We laugh at a man who, stepping out of his room at the very minute when the sun is rising, says, 'It is my will that the sun shall rise'; or at him who, unable to stop a wheel, says, 'I wish it to roll.'"

— Friedrich Nietzsche

Divine one, breathe through me. I am love and light. I am peace and harmony. Divine one, express through me. I am joy and happiness. I am strength and courage. Divine one, surround me with the energetic vibration of all that is good in life, and let it flow outward to everyone I meet today. I am divine. I am one.

Nature has gifts but only for those eyes open enough to see. Even a short walk can be a meditative practice. Notice the green grass, the tall trees, and brightly colored flowers. Listen to people talking, dogs barking, and children playing. Closely observe a butterfly on a leaf or a bee hovering over a rose bush. Look for and see the abundant blessings of nature.

"The less the thought of the body, the better. For it is the body that drags us down. That is the secret: To think that I am the spirit and not the body, and that the whole of this universe with all its relations, with all its good and all its evil, is but as a series of paintings — scenes on a canvas — of which I am the witness."

— Swami Vivekananda

“Man is an infinite circle whose circumference is nowhere, but the centre is located in one spot; and God is an infinite circle whose circumference is nowhere, but whose centre is everywhere. He works through all hands, sees through all eyes, walks on all feet, breathes through all bodies, lives in all life, speaks through every mouth, and thinks through every brain.”

— Swami Vivekananda

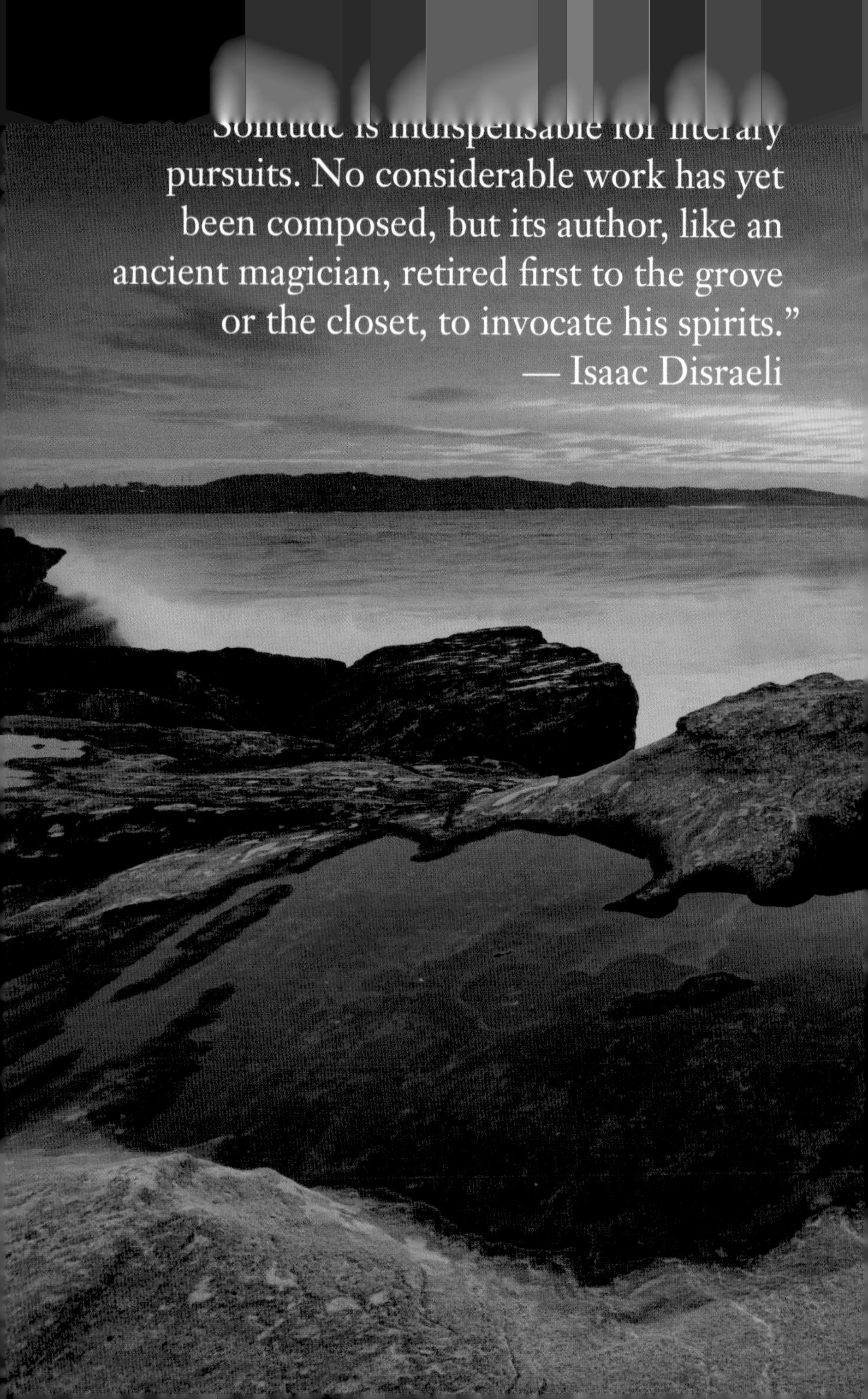
Solitude is indispensable for literary
pursuits. No considerable work has yet
been composed, but its author, like an
ancient magician, retired first to the grove
or the closet, to invocate his spirits."
— Isaac Disraeli

"There is gold buried in your heart, but you are not yet aware of it. It is covered with a thin layer of earth. Once you are aware of it, all these activities of yours will lessen."

— Ramakrishna

Choosing a mantra is a personal exercise in finding the right words, phrase, or saying to resonate with your inner spirit. Try some you've already heard or write one on your own, but be sure it has both meaning and power. Mantras can change as you evolve and grow. Your mantra should help keep your mind focused on a single thought so the body can relax. You may already have a mantra that you repeat without realizing it.

Natalie's young son had a disability that required all of her time and energy. There were doctor appointments and surgeries and rarely did she have even an hour to herself. But she realized she was losing herself to her demanding routine and needed a way to reclaim her mind. She chose to use a mantra, meaningful to only her, and set aside the first five or ten minutes of the day to meditate.

It wasn't much, but those few minutes became her sanctuary amidst the chaos, her stillness in the hurricane of daily life. She felt stronger, centered, and capable. She could be more present for her son and for herself as she supported them both.

"The holiest of all holidays are those
Kept by ourselves in silence and apart;
The secret anniversaries of the heart,
When the full river of feeling overflows."
— Henry Wadsworth Longfellow

We can take a lesson from the precious water lily. For no matter what outside force or pressure is put upon the lily, it always rises back to the water's surface again to feel the nurturing sunlight upon its leaves and petals. We must be like the lily, steadfast and true in the face of every difficulty, that we too may rise above our problems and feel the light on our faces again.

"But he who in solitude adopts no transient feelings, and reflects no artificial lights, who is only himself, possesses an immense advantage: he has not attached importance to what is merely local, but listens to interior truths. He is the man of every age."

— Isaac Disraeli

Sit quietly, eyes closed, and repeat this cycle of mantras to yourself for five minutes:

I am love. I am joy.
I am peace. I am harmony.
I am forgiveness. I am happiness.
I am wholeness. I am healed.
I am balanced. I am love.

Meditate with your eyes open. Find a beautiful piece of visual art that takes you to another place: a photograph, perhaps, or a richly textured oil painting. Let yourself be absorbed in the details of the imagery as you imagine the artist's vision. Close your eyes and be in that place for a while, simply breathing.

"The stars tell all their secrets to the flowers, and, if we only knew how to look around us, we should not need to look above. But man is a plant of slow growth, and great heat is required to bring out his leaves."

— Margaret Fuller

"Solitude is the nurse of enthusiasm, and enthusiasm is the true parent of genius. In all ages solitude has been called for—has been flown to."

— Isaac Disraeli

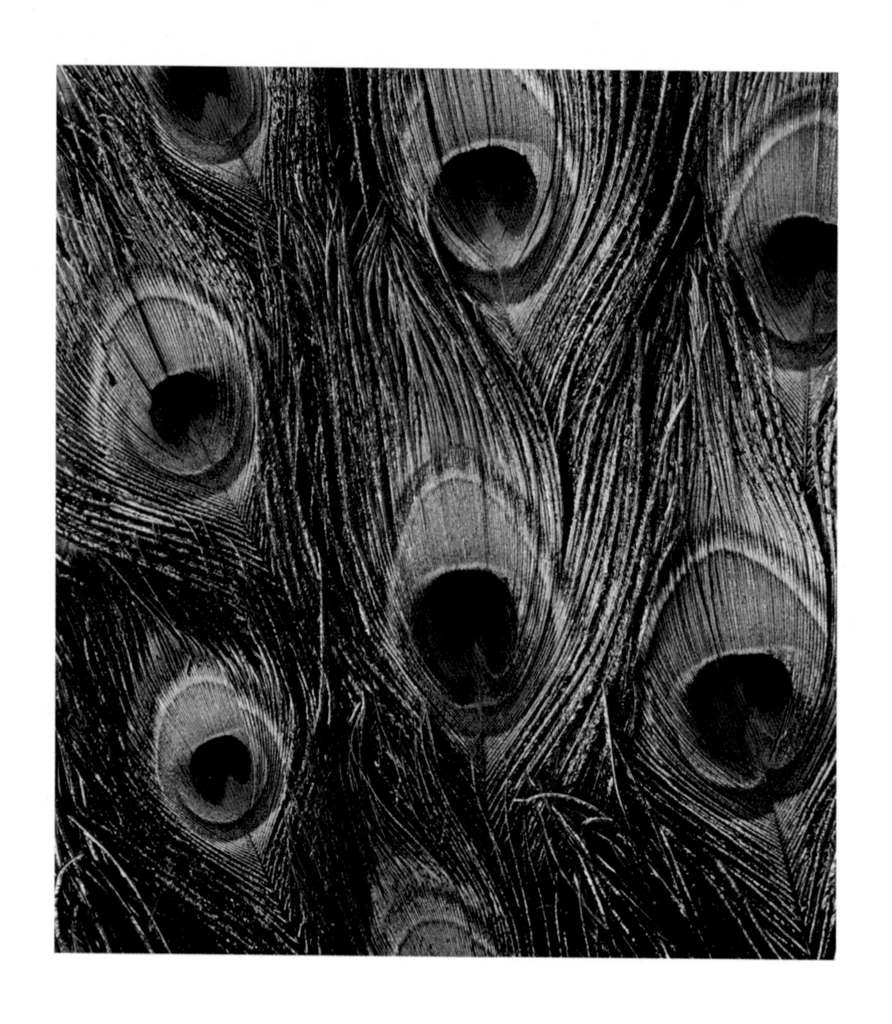

The shorter the mantra, the more powerful it is for keeping the mind focused. “Love,” “I am,” and “I am peace” are examples of brief, effective mantras. Mantras are personal and individual, so find one that fits you and resonates on an intuitive level. Use it daily in your mindfulness practice to stay present.

Being mindful doesn't end when meditation does. It is a way of life that carries over to each challenge, obstacle and situation one encounters. Being mindful means walking through each moment awake to what is, not what should be or has to be. It is letting life flow and not trying to control the direction of that flow.

"If there is dirt and dust on a mirror, we cannot see our image. So ignorance and wickedness are the dirt and dust that are on the mirror of our hearts."

— Swami Vivekananda

There's a place of renewal and happiness within you. All you need to do to reach it is withdraw your attention from the outside world and focus on the strength and the energy inside yourself. A calm spirit pours water on the hottest fire.

Paying attention to my breath, I let go of the need to control. Feeling the rise and fall of my stomach, I release the desire to force things into being. Sitting in stillness with only my thoughts, I give up expectations and allow life to flow like a river through me. Listening in the present, I surrender yesterday and tomorrow.

I sit quietly and let my stress go,
visualizing it washing away from
my body. I breathe, listening to the
sound of air entering and exiting
my lungs, bringing oxygen to my
blood and brain. I continue to let go of
worry, fear, doubt, and regret. In the
present, I simply breathe and
hold onto nothing.

Sit in a crowded place. Look around and absorb every aspect of your environment. See how people rush about. Listen to their chatter. Allow sounds to move through you. You are the observer. Breathe deeply, noticing any smells or sensations. Let them move through you. Be in the chaos, but be still.

How closely do you pay attention to the people you meet each day? Mindfulness teaches us to stay present, because people are often messengers of knowledge or solutions we seek. Look at people, interact with them, talk to them. Be awake and aware of how spirit speaks to us through others.

Often it's our weaknesses that we conceal and feel ashamed of, but these feelings accumulate and poison our spirits. When we find ourselves overwhelmed with feelings of bitterness, it's a signal that we're not devoting enough time to reflection. Our struggles are an opportunity to sit quietly, to breathe deeply, and to exhale these spiritual poisons. What's left will be more fruitful and positive and will have more room to grow.